FORENSIC Investigations

LOST AND FOUND

Looking at Traces of Evidence

Leela Burnscott

Smart Apple Media

Smart Apple Media
P.O. Box 3263
Mankato, MN 56002

First published in 2009 by
MACMILLAN EDUCATION AUSTRALIA PTY LTD
15–19 Claremont Street, South Yarra 3141

Visit our website at www.macmillan.com.au or go directly to www.macmillanlibrary.com.au

Associated companies and representatives throughout the world.

Library of Congress Cataloging-in-Publication Data

Burnscott, Leela.
    Lost and found: looking at traces of evidence / Leela Burnscott.
       p. cm. — (Forensic investigations)
    Includes index.
    ISBN 978-1-59920-461-1 (hardcover)
    1. Evidence, Criminal—Juvenile literature. 2. Criminal investigation—Juvenile literature. 3. Forensic sciences—Juvenile literature.
    4. Crime scene searches—Juvenile literature. I. Title.
    HV8073.8.B868 2010
    363.25'62--dc22

                                                                    2009003449

Edited by Georgina Garner
Text and cover design by Cristina Neri, Canary Graphic Design
Page layout by Raul Diche
Photo research by Sarah Johnson
Illustrations by Alan Laver, Shelly Communications

Printed in the United States

Acknowledgments
The author and the publisher are grateful to the following for permission to reproduce copyright material:

Front cover photograph: Collecting paint evidence. Forensic scientist collecting a paint sample from part of a car. He is using a microscope to look for tiny traces of paint left by a collision with another car. Comparison of the paint with known paint samples can aid identification of the other vehicle © Mauro Fermariello/Science Photo Library/Photolibrary

Background images used throughout pages: fingerprint courtesy of iStockphoto/James Steidl; tweezers courtesy of iStockphoto/Mitar Holod; forensic investigation kit courtesy of iStockphoto/Brandon Alms.

Images courtesy of: © Bettmann/Corbis, **7**; Getty Images/Chad Ehlers, **17**; Getty Images/Dan Trevan/AFP, **4**; Getty Images/G. Wanner, **11** (top right); Getty Images/Neil Fletcher and Matthew Ward, **27** (bottom); Getty Images/Simko, **11** (bottom left); Getty Images/Spike Walker, **10**; iStockphoto, **18** (bottom right), **26**, **30** (middle left and top right); iStockphoto/Andrey Milkin, **27** (top); iStockphoto/Bart Coenders, **21**; iStockphoto/Egor Mopanko, **19** (top); iStockphoto/George Bailey, **18** (bottom left); iStockphoto/Kristin Smith, **18** (top); iStockphoto/Pamela Moore, **30** (top left); iStockphoto/Ron Bailey, **18** (middle); iStockphoto/Tim Buckner, **19** (bottom); iStockphoto/Vaide Dambrauskaite, **15**; iStockphoto/Yvonne Chamberlain, **6**; Sarah Johnson, **16**; Renae Payne/Newsphotos, **29**; Andrew Syred/Science Photo Library/Photolibrary, **11** (middle right); Colin Cuthbert/Science Photo Library/Photolibrary, **30** (bottom right); Dr Jeremy Burgess/Science Photo Library/Photolibrary, **20**; Dr Keith Wheeler/Science Photo Library/Photolibrary, **22**; Klaus Guldbrandsen/Science Photo Library/Photolibrary, **28**; Martyn F. Chillmaid/Science Photo Library/Photolibrary, **27** (middle); Mauro Fermariello/Science Photo Library/Photolibrary, **5**, **12**, **24**, **25**; Philippe Psaila/Science Photo Library/Photolibrary, **30** (bottom left); Steve Gschmeissner/Science Photo Library/Photolibrary, **11** (bottom right); Susumu Nishinaga/Science Photo Library/Photolibrary, **13** (both), **14**; Tek Image/Science Photo Library/Photolibrary, **9**; Shutterstock/Dole, **23**; Image copyright © Victorian Institute of Forensic Medicine, **30** (middle right).

Text reference: Hugh Miller (1991). *Indelible Evidence: An International Collection of True Crimes which have been Solved by Forensic Science*, Crows Nest, NSW, Australia: ABC Enterprises, **28–9** (background information)

The publisher advises that the names in the case study on pages 28–9 have been changed.

While every care has been taken to trace and acknowledge copyright, the publisher tenders their apologies for any accidental infringement where copyright has proved untraceable. Where the attempt has been unsuccessful, the publisher welcomes information that would redress the situation.

Contents

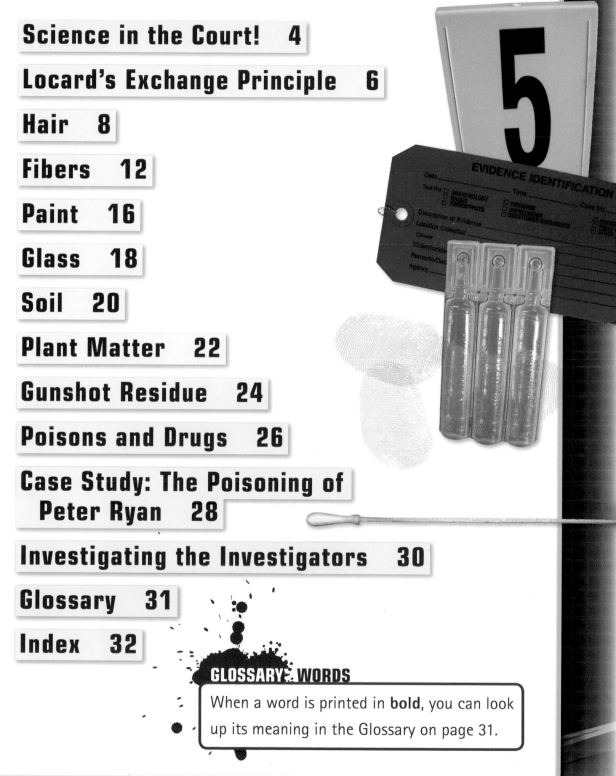

Science in the Court! 4

Locard's Exchange Principle 6

Hair 8

Fibers 12

Paint 16

Glass 18

Soil 20

Plant Matter 22

Gunshot Residue 24

Poisons and Drugs 26

Case Study: The Poisoning of
    Peter Ryan 28

Investigating the Investigators 30

Glossary 31

Index 32

GLOSSARY WORDS

When a word is printed in **bold**, you can look up its meaning in the Glossary on page 31.

Science in the Court!

Forensic science is the use of scientific knowledge and techniques within the legal system, particularly in the investigation of crime. Forensic science can:

- determine if an **incident** resulted from an accident, natural causes, or a criminal act
- identify those involved in the incident
- identify and find those people responsible for the incident
- make sure that the innocent are not wrongly convicted

The term "forensic science" is quite misleading because it suggests only one type of science is involved. This is certainly not the case. Forensic investigations can involve virtually every field of science and technology, from electronics to psychology.

Forensic investigations require the skills of specially trained police, scientists, doctors, engineers, and other professionals. These investigators examine all types of evidence, from bloodstains to weapons and from bugs to computers. The greater the pool of evidence against an accused person, the greater the chance of a conviction.

A forensic expert presents crime scene photographs during a trial.

Lost and Found

Forensic investigators are excellent at finding things that people lose, especially those things they accidentally leave behind. Every time people or objects come into contact with each other, material from each one is transferred to the other. This principle was first described by Frenchman Edmond Locard, who was one of the founders of forensic science in the early 1900s.

This type of material that is recovered from crime scenes, weapons, suspects, and victims is called trace evidence. Trace evidence can be hairs, fibers, paint, dirt, blood, and anything else that can pass from one object to another. The value of trace evidence is that it can link a person to a scene, object, or both. Once forensic investigators get their hands on trace evidence, stories can be unravelled and crimes solved.

An investigator searches for trace evidence left in the trunk of a car.

Locard's Exchange Principle

Edmond Locard studied crime scene evidence in France in the early 1900s. He discovered that every time a person visits a place or comes in contact with another person, they leave something of themselves behind, either at the place or on the other person. In the same way, they take away something from the place or the other person. This theory became known as the Locard Exchange Principle and led to forensic trace evidence detection. It became one of the most important forensic theories and helped establish the field of forensic science.

Paul Leland Kirk was an American scientist who followed and promoted Locard's Exchange Principle from the 1930s to the 1960s. He helped improve the detection and collection of trace evidence and strengthened Locard's Exchange Principle. Kirk became a leading figure in forensic science in America.

When a dog and a child come in contact with each other, the dog leaves trace material, such as dog hairs, on the child and the child leaves trace material, such as her hair, on the dog.

Edmond Locard

Edmond Locard was born in France in 1877 and died in 1966. During the early 1900s, he found ways of involving scientific practices in the fight against crime. He based a lot of his work on ideas and research carried out by Austrian scientist Hans Gross (1847–1915). Locard has been described as a real-life Sherlock Holmes or super sleuth.

In 1910, Locard started the world's first police laboratory. It was made up of himself, two assistants, an old microscope, and a few other pieces of equipment. Locard wrote many forensic science papers, such as one that established the original standard of 12 matching points for fingerprint identification.

Some suspects readily confessed to their crimes when they were confronted with Locard's evidence. His success led to the establishment of police laboratories throughout Europe and throughout the rest of the world.

Edmond Locard was one of the world's first forensic investigators.

DID YOU KNOW?

In more recent times, America's Federal Bureau of Investigation (FBI) has led the world in major improvements in forensic techniques.

Hair

Although hair is not unique like a fingerprint, it can be matched to its owner. Hair can also provide information about a person's age, sex, race, and health.

Examining Hair

Forensic investigators use a variety of microscopes to look at different characteristics of hairs. Different microscopes magnify the hairs to reveal different small details. These details can help investigators work out:

- which species the hair comes from
- if the hair is dyed or naturally colored
- if the hair was removed with force or if it fell out naturally
- if the person it came from was poisoned

When the **hair sheath** is still attached, the owner's DNA can often be recovered.

Under the Microscope

A strand of hair is made up of different layers. The characteristics of each layer help in hair identification and comparison.

The cuticle is the outer layer. Just under the cuticle is the cortex layer. The cells of the cortex determine a person's natural hair color. The inner-most layer of hair is called the medulla.

Not all hairs have a medulla. Thin, young hair often does not have this layer, and as hair ages it loses its medulla.

The cuticle is made up of tiny, overlapping scales.

The cortex is made up of spindle-shaped cells.

The medulla is made up of rows of cells stacked on top of each other.

Human hair is made up of three different layers.

A forensic investigator examines hair evidence.

DID YOU KNOW?

People once thought that hair continued to grow after death, because a corpse appears to have longer hair than when the person died. The hair just looks longer, however, because the skin and flesh of the face has dried out and shrunk.

Hair Evidence

Humans shed hair naturally but hair is also pulled out or broken off when people scuffle. This is why hairs are often found at crime scenes.

Hairs are almost indestructible and they do not decompose quickly like flesh can. This means that hair can be recovered from badly decomposed bodies or from a weapon years after an incident. Fire, some chemicals, and cockroaches are about the only things that can destroy hair.

Proving a Struggle

Often, a suspect will admit to being involved in an incident in which a person was hurt or killed, but claim that it was an accident and no force was used. Looking at hairs is one way to find out if a suspect is telling the truth.

A thin layer of cells, called a sheath, forms at the base of each hair root. This hardly ever comes out when hair falls out naturally. Finding sheaths on hairs at the scene indicates that the hair was pulled out with force. This suggests that a struggle took place and the suspect is lying.

Even though hairs can naturally break in two, this does not normally happen in great numbers. If lots of small broken bits of hair are found, this too suggests that a struggle took place or that force was used.

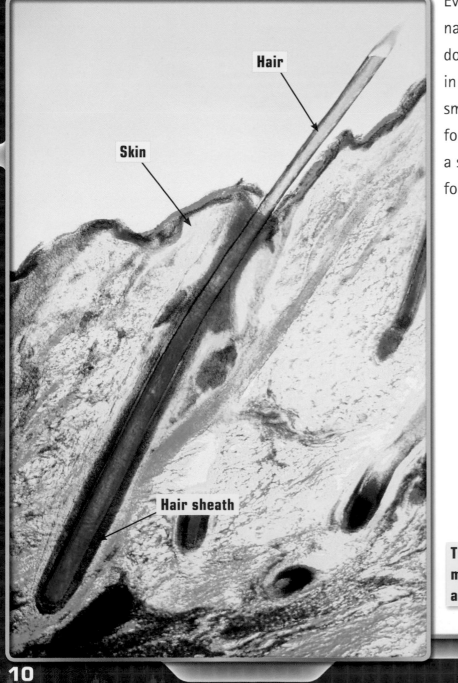

Hair

Skin

Hair sheath

The human scalp can be magnified to show the hair and hair sheath.

Poisons and Colorings

The cortex of hair is like a sponge and absorbs chemicals, especially poisons, from the body. Scientists can extract the chemicals from the hair and identify them to help discover the cause of death. In cases of arsenic poisoning, the hair is one of the few parts of the body where traces of the chemical can be found.

The cortex absorbs dyes easily, too. By looking at hair under a microscope, experts can tell if it has been dyed or bleached.

Identifying Different Species

Each species of animal, including humans, has a fairly unique sheath and medulla. Human hairs have very small, narrow medullae, and a rabbit's medulla looks like corn on a cob. By examining the sheath scales and medulla cell arrangements of hairs, the species that the hair came from can be discovered.

Cat hair, as seen under a microscope

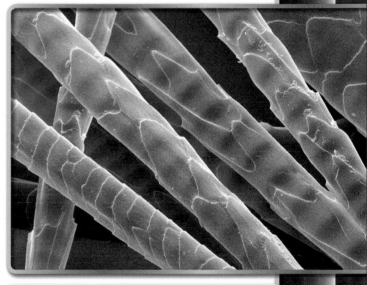
Mouse hair, as seen under a microscope

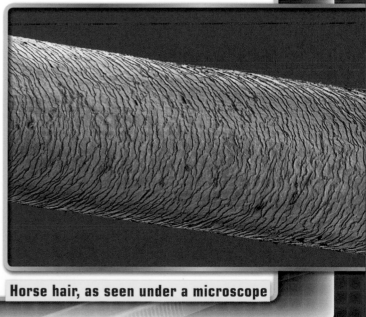
Horse hair, as seen under a microscope

Human hair, as seen under a microscope

11

Fibers

Fibers are extremely valuable pieces of forensic evidence. Fibers are small threads that can come from objects such as rope, hessian bags, clothing, carpet, curtains, and blankets.

Fiber Evidence

Fiber evidence is often found at a crime scene and on the bodies of victims and offenders. It can link a suspect to a crime or link two crimes together. Fibers can also be used to discover artwork fraud.

Fibers can naturally break off materials through normal wear and tear. Fibers and pieces of material can also rip off:

- during a struggle
- when caught on an object, such as a nail or twig
- when hit with great force

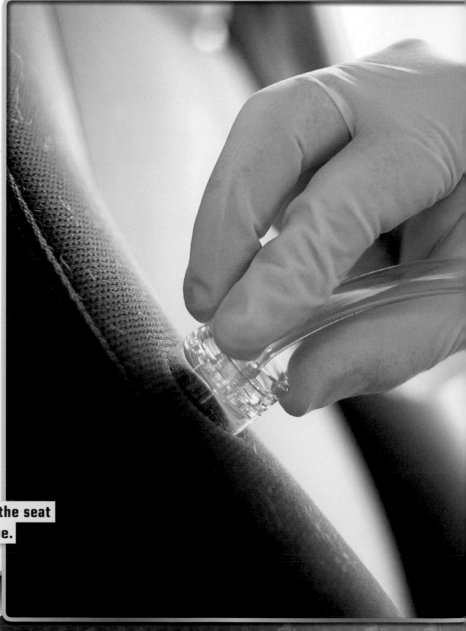

CASE NOTE

When a person is hit by a car, fibers from their clothing can get trapped on the car's undercarriage, hood, windshield wipers, or license plate. This trace evidence could be used to link a car to an accident.

Fiber evidence is collected from the seat of a car using a small suction tube.

Types of Fibers

The two main types of fibers are natural and **synthetic**. Natural fibers are those that are made from plant or animal materials, such as wool, silk, and cotton. Synthetic fibers do not contain plant or animal material. Nylon, rayon, lycra, and polyester are synthetic fibers. Synthetic fibers were first mass-produced in the early 1900s. They are now the most widely used fibers in the rope, fabric, and carpet industries.

Under the Microscope

Natural fibers look very different from synthetic fibers under a microscope. Animal fibers such as wool are in fact hairs, so they have a sheath, cortex and medulla. Plant materials such as cotton have a distinctive, twisted ribbon-like shape. Synthetic fibers look very different to natural fibers and to each other.

Some synthetic fibers have very smooth surfaces.

Under a microscope, it is obvious that natural fibers such as wool are hairs.

Examining Fibers

Different fibers and materials have different characteristics. Their physical characteristics can be detected by looking at them under a microscope. Characteristics include:

- overall shape
- thickness
- marks, grooves, or other **striations**
- number of strands
- type of strands

Synthetic fibers can have chemical characteristics that come from:

- the dye lot used to color the fiber
- chemical treatments, such as the use of titanium oxide to reduce shine
- the chemical compounds that make up the synthetic fiber

Chemical analysis involves techniques such as infrared spectrophotometry and chromatography. Infrared spectrophotometry involves measuring the different wavelengths of light reflected by the fiber. Chromatography involves extracting and separating the dyes in the fiber.

The weave pattern of a piece of ripped material can be examined to try to match it to a specific item of clothing. The piece itself can be fitted to a tear in a garment, a bit like fitting jigsaw pieces together.

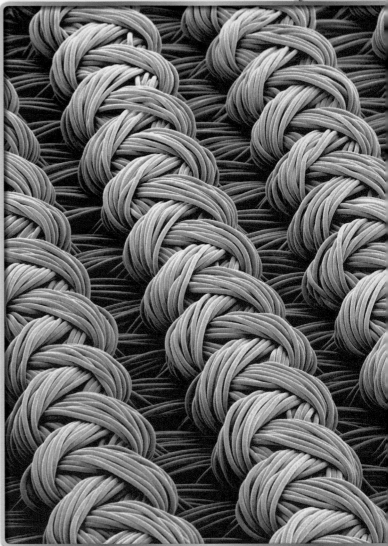

Under a microscope, the woven threads that make up a piece of material can be seen.

DID YOU KNOW?

Materials are made from woven threads. Each thread can be made up of two or more individual strands twisted or plaited together. These strands can be a mix of synthetic and natural fibers.

Problems with Fiber Evidence

Today, most materials are made in huge quantities and sold all around the world. There could be tens of thousands of items made out of the one roll of fabric. This makes it almost impossible for a fiber expert to match a crime-scene fiber to the specific item it came from.

Fibers and Fraud

Copies of paintings are sometimes accidentally or purposely sold as originals. To check if a painting is **authentic**, experts test fibers from the painting's canvas. If modern canvas fibers are found in a painting that is said to come from the 1800s, then the painting must be a fraud. The authenticity of ancient artifacts can also be tested in this way.

CASE NOTE

If a green polyester fiber is found at a crime scene and the suspect is found to own a green polyester shirt, this does not prove that the fiber came from the suspect's shirt. More evidence is needed to link the suspect and that particular shirt to the crime.

Fabrics are mass-produced and sold around the world.

Paint

Paint is one of the most common pieces of trace evidence. It can easily transfer to a person's clothing or tools as they force open a window or it can be left on a car when another car hits it.

Paint Evidence

Paint is made up of three main parts:

- pigments, which are the chemicals that give a paint its color
- binders, which bind the pigments together and allow them to stick to surfaces
- solvents, which keep a paint in liquid form until it is painted onto a surface, and the solvent evaporates and the paint hardens and dries

Other things are added too, such as metallic flakes that alter the **sheen** of the paints. These additives and the binder are what makes a paint acrylic, lacquer, enamel, or water-based, and what gives the paint its sheen type, such as gloss or metallic.

Swatches show paints of different colors, sheens, and textures.

Analyzing Paint

Paints come in many colors, forms, and sheens. There are thousands of different pigment–binder mixes, making it easy to differentiate between paints. Each combination of pigments and binders absorbs and reflects light differently. Forensic chemists use specialized equipment to measure these differences and identify and compare different paints.

Car paint is applied in layers, and each layer has special characteristics and properties. Car manufacturers often use a different series of paint layers for different models and change the color range each year. Investigators are often able to pinpoint the make and model of the car that a paint flake came from.

When a house is repainted, the layering of the different paints produces a paint profile of that house. This helps investigators match paint flakes found on either tools or a suspect to a house that was broken into.

Cars of the same model made on the same assembly line are spray-painted with the same paint.

DID YOU KNOW?

Light is made up of a spectrum of different wavelengths: violet, indigo, blue, green, yellow, orange, and red. When all the wavelengths are absorbed by a pigment or dye, an object appears black. When all but the red wavelength is absorbed, the object appears red because the red light wavelength is reflected back.

Glass

Glass comes in different forms, such as window glass, pyrex, plate, toughened, laminated, and ceramic. Glass can be tinted, colored, etched, patterned, **opaque**, or semi-opaque.

Types of Glass

Most glass is one of the following four chemical types:

- Soda-lime glass is the most common glass. It is used for regular window glass.
- Borosilicate glass can withstand high heat. It is used for ovenware and laboratory glassware.
- Aluminosilicate glass is a tough glass that can withstand extremely hot and cold temperature. It is used for aircraft windows.
- Lead glass is a very heavy glass also known as crystal. Crystal is ideal for engraving. It is often used in glass artworks and to make fancy drinking glasses.

Forensic chemists use a number of techniques to work out the type of glass. They also detect other identifiable chemicals within the glass, such as pigments.

Windows are made from soda-lime glass.

Pyrex is a kind of borosilicate glass used for oven dishes.

Crystal items, such as this crystal globe, are often engraved with artwork or patterns.

An aircraft window is made from aluminosilicate glass.

Physical Characteristics of Glass

Some of the physical characteristics of glass are:

- the strength of the glass, such as whether it breaks easily
- the way the glass breaks, such as shattering or cracking vertically, horizontally, or radially
- its optical properties, such as the way it reflects light
- any patterns, markings, or logos.

By examining its physical characteristics, a forensic investigator can determine the type of glass and where it is likely to have come from. By comparing a fragment of glass to its possible source, the investigator can determine if, in fact, it is a match.

A drinking glass breaks into large pieces.

The glass in a car window is treated so that it shatters into small pieces, rather than breaking into large dangerous pieces.

Soil

The composition of soil can be dramatically different across a very small area. Soil is excellent for linking a suspect or an object to a crime or crime scene.

Composition of Soil

Soil is composed of minerals and salts mixed with almost anything that falls onto or seeps into the ground. Oil from a leaking car, fertilizers used on a garden, rust from an old metal pipe, and soot from a forest fire can all be found in soil.

Some of the most common components of soil samples are:

- plant remains, seeds, and pollens
- animal remains and waste
- fossils
- spores
- microbes, such as bacteria and fungi
- chemicals
- solid **contaminants** and rubbish

Under a microscope, the mix of things that make up a soil sample can be seen.

Analyzing Soil

Forensic examiners may work with tiny flecks or large containers of soil. Tiny samples are often recovered from car tyres or shoes. Larger samples come directly from the crime scene.

Soil analysis can involve many steps and different techniques.

One of the first steps is to remove large objects from the soil. For large samples, this can be done by filtering the soil. For small samples, the investigator may use a microscope and physically pick out any contaminants.

Any insect material should then be examined by an **entomologist**, and plant material should be studied by a **botanist**. Solid contaminants, such as glass, paper, plastics, and coins, could be examined by fingerprint experts, document examiners, or chemists.

Next, a small sample of the soil is taken for chemical analysis. This reveals what minerals and salts make up the soil and in what quantities. All this information can pinpoint where the soil came from.

A forensic examiner sifts through soil samples, searching for contaminants.

DO NOT CROSS — CRIME SCENE — DO NOT CR

Plant Matter

Plant matter includes pollen, seeds, leaves, bark, twigs, and wood. These materials can fix themselves unnoticed in clothing, hair, car tyres, and other objects.

Physical Characteristics of Plant Matter

Pollen, seeds, and leaves of different plant species differ greatly in size, shape, structure, and texture. They can be hard or soft, thin or thick, smooth or prickly, plain, or covered in fine hairs. Woods differ in color, odor, ring growth patterns, **pores**, and **resin canals**. Processed timbers also differ in their chemical treatments.

Some of the differences between plant matter can be easily seen, but most need microscopic examination. Using a plant's physical characteristics, investigators can help:

- prove or disprove a person's story
- link a person to a scene
- determine a person's movements
- identify a weapon, such as a wooden stake or bat
- link a tool, car, or room to a crime
- determine where and when an incident happened
- determine where a victim or weapon was dumped

A plant burr hooks itself onto a woolen jumper.

anther

petal

pollen

Each type of flower has a different type of pollen.

Where the Plant Matter Came From

Although some plants can grow in a variety of areas, most are restricted to certain soil types, climate zones, and weather conditions. If trace evidence comes from a plant that is uncommon or has a small growth area, this can help narrow down the places it could come from.

When the Plant Matter Was Picked Up

The life cycle of plants can be the key to determining what time of year an incident happened. This is because plants sprout, flower, pollinate, and go to seed according to seasons and local weather conditions. Finding pollen that comes from a winter-flowering plant on the clothes of a buried body discovered in spring indicates that the body was most likely buried during winter.

Gunshot Residue

Gunshot residue is a fine film of powder released when a gun is fired. This residue is easily chemically "fingerprinted" and can be used to link a gun and a shooter to a crime.

Location of Gunshot Residue

When the trigger of a gun is pulled, it causes the gunpowder in the bullet to explode. This releases gunshot residue into the air. Some residue can be seen, but most cannot. Experts look for it in places such as:

- on the gun itself
- on the bullet and its cartridge case
- on the hands of the shooter
- on the clothes and shoes of the shooter
- on nearby objects
- on the target that was shot, if it is close enough

If the gun is not thoroughly cleaned, the residue can be transferred to anyone else who handles the gun and to the object that the gun is stored in.

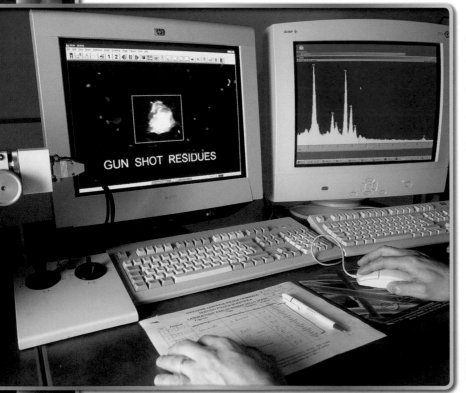

A ballistics expert analyzes a gunshot residue pattern.

Gunshot Residue Patterns

Where the gunshot residue falls tells many important things about the crime, such as:

- the distance between the gun and the target
- the bullet size, called the bullet's caliber
- the type of gunpowder
- the type of gun and its barrel length

Knowing the distance between the target and the shooter is very important. This information can determine if the shooting was accidental or intentional, and carried out by the victim or another person. Knowing the type of gun or bullets used can help police find the weapon and link the culprit to the crime.

Collecting Gunshot Residue

Several methods are used to collect gunshot residue. One involves "lifting" the residue with adhesive tape. Another method involves swabbing or washing the object with water or dilute acid. A third option is to vacuum the surface using a specially designed vacuum-filter.

Gunshot residue is collected from a suspect's hand.

Poisons and Drugs

Hunting down traces of poisons or drugs in a person, food, or drink is the job of a forensic toxicologist.

Detecting Poisons and Drugs

The detection of poisons or drugs is often a difficult task. Many poisons and drugs are naturally cleared from the body within days. Others can only be detected in high **concentrations** or only in certain body tissues or fluids.

Normally, the first poison or drug screens conducted are blood and urine tests. When a person has died, their tissue, organs, bones, nails, and hair can be screened as well. Bones, nails, and hair are the main areas where drugs and poisons build up over time and remain at detectable levels.

CASE NOTE

More than 170 years after the death of German composer Ludwig van Beethoven (1770–1827), high concentrations of lead were found in his skull bones and samples of his hair. Forensic scientists believe that he died of accidental, long-term lead poisoning. Lead was widely used in the 1700s and 1800s before its dangers were known.

Beethoven died from years of lead poisoning at the age of 57.

Poisons, Drugs, and Crime

Just because traces of poisons or drugs are found does not automatically mean **foul play** was involved. The poisoning or drugging could have been accidental or self-inflicted. Generally, when foul play is to blame, poisons are used to kill or make a person very ill. Drugs are not only used to kill, but also to sedate or knock someone out.

Self-administered drugs such as alcohol and marijuana make drivers drive erratically and cause car accidents. Some prescription medications and most illegal drugs, such as speed or heroin, can alter a person's mind, causing them to become violent, frantic, or confused. This can lead them to harm themselves or injure or kill others. Some normally safe prescription medications can cause mood swings and dangerous behavior when mixed with alcohol or other medications. Forensic investigators need to check for all these things.

Arsenic is a poisonous chemical that comes from the earth.

Lead is a poisonous metal that comes from the earth.

CASE NOTE

Breathalyzers measure alcohol levels in breath, but these tests are not admissible as evidence. Anyone whose breathalyzer reading is over the legal limit must also give a blood sample for testing. The driver will be arrested for drunk driving only if the blood alcohol level is above the legal limit.

Strychnine is a poison that comes from the strychnine plant.

The Poisoning of Peter Ryan

Background

Peter Ryan lived with his wife Susan and his three children near Bendigo in Victoria, Australia. He was a healthy, fit man who worked as a butcher. In 1978, he suddenly became very ill. This was the start of a six-year illness. None of the 50 doctors who examined him over this period could work out why he was so ill. Between June 1983 and January 1984, Peter's health got worse and he eventually became an invalid. During these 15 months, he was admitted to hospital five times. He died in hospital on January 14, 1984, aged 38.

The Crime

It was not until the autopsy that the authorities found out what had caused Peter's illness and death. He had died from toxic levels of lead arsenic. This poison is widely used in rat poisons and insecticides. It had caused Peter's constant bouts of vomiting, bloody diarrhea, stomach cramps, sweats, fevers, hallucinations, rashes, blisters, and fits.

The coroner believed that Peter's high levels of arsenic could not have been caused by accidental poisoning. Peter had either been poisoning himself or someone else had poisoned him. After a long investigation, his wife was charged with his murder on July 6, 1986.

Peter Ryan was poisoned using arsenic powder.

The Evidence

The autopsy revealed Peter's urine contained 53 times the normal level of arsenic. Arsenic levels in his blood were 20 times the normal amount.

Arsenic profiles of Peter's hair showed that he had been **ingesting** arsenic since at least 1982. He had one extremely high dose in October–November 1983 and another in January 1984. The coroner stated that in January 1984 Peter was so disabled that he could not have taken the arsenic himself. This suggested murder.

The evidence that led to his wife's arrest was only **circumstantial** and she was found not guilty of Peter's murder. The circumstantial evidence was that:

Susan Ryan was imprisoned for the murder of her husband.

- traces of lead arsenic powder were found in a food container hidden in the family's garage

- Peter's workmates stated that Peter would often complain that his lunch, which was left-overs, tasted awful but had been great the night before when everyone else ate it

- on two occasions, Peter was so ill he could not eat, so he gave his lunch away. Both times, the workmate who ate his lunch became violently ill for weeks

In 2002, Susan Ryan was again tried for the murder of her husband. This time she was convicted and sentenced to 22 years in jail. The evidence that led to her re-arrest was her confession. Susan had confessed to her daughter in 2000 because she mistakenly thought that she could not be convicted of a crime committed more than 15 years previously.

Investigating the Investigators

Most forensic investigators are police members with a science, engineering, or other relevant university degree. Outside experts are also involved. The following investigators are just some of the experts involved in examining trace evidence.

Botanists

Botanists study plants. They can specialize in many fields, such as plant anatomy, biology, or chemistry.

Geologists

Geologists specialize in the study of the structure and composition of soil and rocks. They are often used for forensic soil analysis.

Chemists

Chemists specialize in the various fields of chemistry. They are not pharmacists, who are sometimes also called chemists. Chemists work in many fields in forensic science, from paint analysis to soil analysis.

Forensic Pathologists

Forensic pathologists are medical doctors who specialize in carrying out autopsies. Their main role is to determine how, when, and where a person died, but they also examine wounds on surviving victims. Pathologists often examine bloodstain patterns at the crime scene.

Entomologists

Entomologists study insects. They can specialize in fields such as insect anatomy, biology, behavior, or life cycles.

Toxicologists

Toxicologists measure levels of chemicals, such as drugs and poisons, in living systems.

Glossary

authentic	genuine
botanist	scientist who studies plants
circumstantial	pointing towards someone's guilt, but not proving it
concentrations	amounts of a substance within another substance
contaminants	impurities in something
entomologist	scientist who studies insects
foul play	behavior that is against the law
hair sheath	thin layer of cells that surrounds the hair root
incident	violent, dangerous, or criminal event
ingesting	taking food or drink by swallowing it
opaque	not able to be seen through
pores	tiny openings in a surface
resin canals	tubes that hold resin, which is the fluid produced by plants to seal up wounds and carry nutrients
sheen	shine of an object
striations	long parallel lines or ridges
synthetic	man-made, not naturally produced

Index

A
aluminosilicate glass 18
animal fibers 13
animal hair 11
arsinic 11, 27, 28, 29
artifacts 15
autopsy 28, 29, 30

B
Beethoven, Ludwig van 26
binders 16, 17
blood alcohol level 27
blood tests 26, 27
borosilicate glass 18
botanists 21, 30
breathalyzers 27
bullets 24, 25

C
car accidents 12, 16, 27
chemicals 9, 11, 14, 16, 18, 20, 21, 22, 30
chemists 17, 18, 21, 30
cortex 8, 11, 13
crime scene 5, 6, 9, 12, 15, 20, 21, 30
crystal 18
cuticle 8

D
DNA 8
drunk driving 27
drugs 26–27, 30
dye 8, 11, 14, 17

E
entomologists 21, 30
evidence 4, 5, 6, 7, 9, 12, 15, 16, 23, 27, 29

F
Federal Bureau of Investigation (FBI) 7
fibers 5, 12–15
fingerprints 7, 8
forensic investigators 5, 8, 19, 27, 30
foul play 27
fraud 12, 15

G
geologists 30
glass 18–19, 21
Gross, Hans 7
gunpowder 24, 25
gunshot residue 24–25

H
hair 5, 6, 8–11, 13, 22, 26, 29
hair sheaths 8, 10, 11, 13

K
Kirk, Paul Leland 6

L
lead glass 18
leaves 22
life cycles 23, 30
light 14, 17, 19
Locard, Edmond 5, 6, 7
Locard's Exchange Principle 5, 6–7

M
medulla 8, 11, 13

N
natural fibers 13, 14

P
paint 5, 16–17, 30
paintings 15
pathologists 30
pigments 16, 17, 18
plants 13, 20, 21, 22, 23, 30
poisons 11, 26–27, 28, 30
police laboratories 7
pollen 20, 22, 23
pool of evidence 4
prescription medications 27

S
seeds 20, 22, 23
sheath 8, 10, 11, 13
soda-lime glass 18
soil 20–21, 23, 30
species identification 11
striations 14
synthetic fibers 13, 14

T
threads 12, 14
toxicologists 26, 30
trace evidence 5, 6, 12, 16, 23, 30

U
urine test 26

W
weave pattern 14
wood 22